Published by Arcadia Children's Books
A Division of Arcadia Publishing
Charleston, SC
www.arcadiapublishing.com

First published 2021

Manufactured in the United States

ISBN 978-1-4671-9842-4

Library of Congress Control Number: 2021938396

All images used © Shutterstock.com; p. 20-21 Leena Robinson/
Shutterstock.com; p. 49 PiercarloAbate/Shutterstock.
com; pp. 94-95 Patrish Jackson/Shutterstock.com.

Cover illustration: Craig Yoe
Design: Jessica Nevins

Craig Yoe has written a TON of kids'
joke books! Yoe has been a creative
director for Nickelodeon, Disney, and
Jim Henson at the Muppets. Raised
in the Midwest, he has lived from
New York to California and has six kids!

CONTENTS

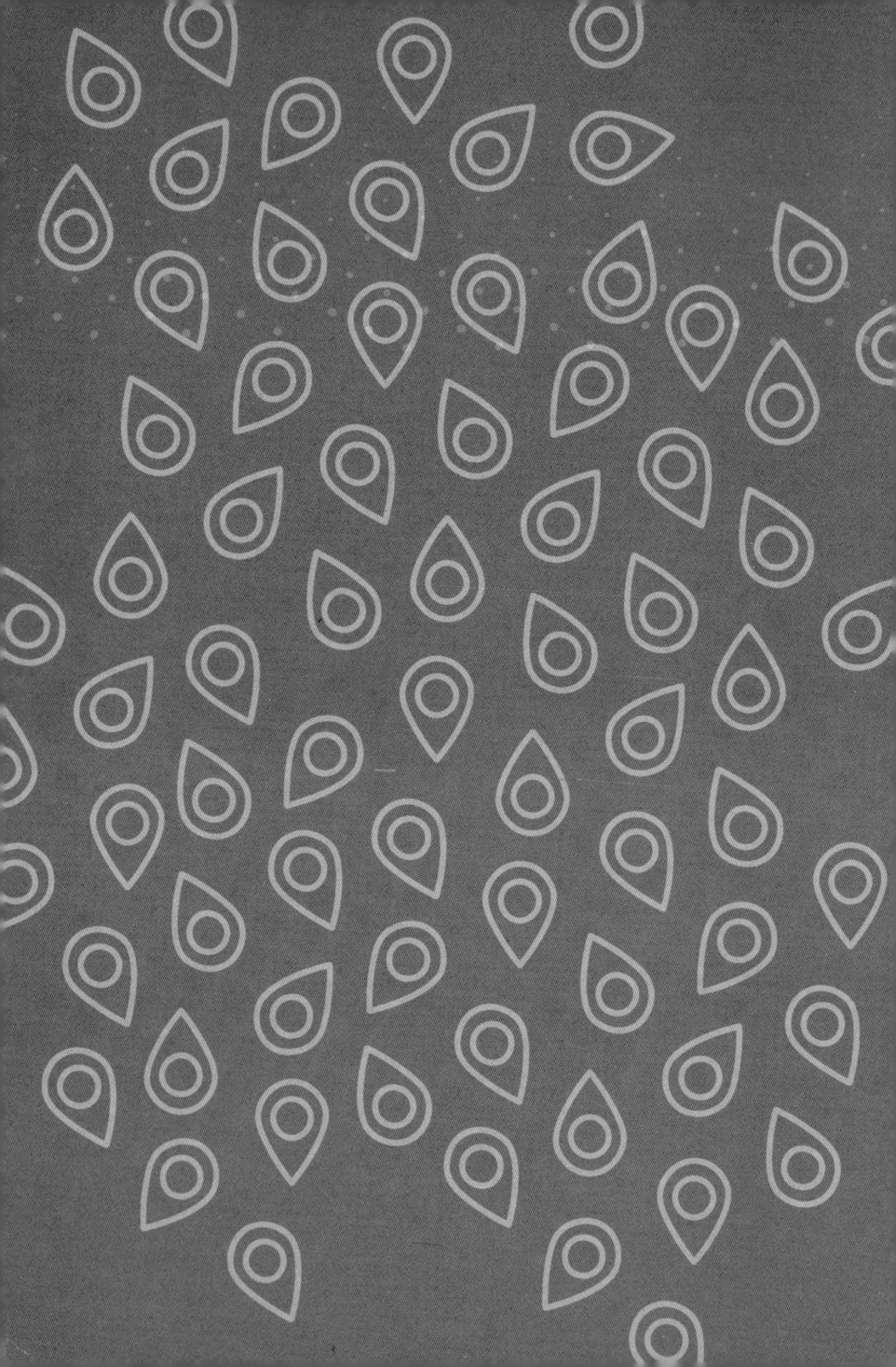

KNOCK! KNOCK!

WHO'S THERE?
Ya!

YA WHO?
I'm pleased as pie to see you, too!

What did the cowboy say at his second rodeo? **"THIS AIN'T MY FIRST RODEO!"**

What kind of shoes did the ghost cowgirl wear to the hoedown?

BOOOO-TS!

Dinosaur + Cowboy = ...?

TYRANNOSAURUS TEX

A+! ☺

Why did the cowgirl get an "A" on her math test?

She was good as all get out at **ROUNDING UP!**

Isabella:

¿Cómo se llama el vaquero a su hija?

Ignacio:

¡HiJAAAAAAA!

What did the cowgirl think about the campfire?

She gave it a **GLOWING** review!

Where do cowboys feed their herd?

The **CALF**-eteria!

How did the cowgirl become so rich?

Her horse gave her lots of bucks every day!

Tyler: By golly, how do you count that many cattle?

Beth: With a COW-culator!

What did Obi-Wan say at the rodeo?

"USE THE HORSE, LUKE!"

THE TEXAS NAME GAME!

The big state of Texas has lots of small towns with wacky names! These are the *nicest* sounding towns in the Lone Star State:

HAPPY, Texas

FRIENDSHIP, Texas

BLANKET, Texas

BLESSING, Texas

RAINBOW, Texas

SMILEY, Texas

Does the name of this Texas town ring a bell?: **DiNG DONG**, Texas

If you had your druthers would y'all want to live in: **BEST**, Texas, or . . . **VERiBEST**, Texas?

Don't be confused, but there's also:
PiTTSBURGH, Texas
MiAMi, Texas
DETROiT, Texas

Not to mention:
EGYPT, Texas
CHiNA, Texas
PALESTiNE, Texas
iTALY, Texas
and even **EARTH**, Texas!

And this Tex town is out of this world:

VENUS, Texas!

Watch yer step in: **BiGFOOT**, Texas

or **MULESHOE**, Texas

Looking for a fight?
Then go to: **BUG TUSSLE**, Texas

You might be lost if
you find yourself in:
UNCERTAIN, Texas,
or . . .

NOWHERE,
Texas!

One last bit of nutty nomenclature:
A town in Denton County used to
be called Clark. The Dish Network
satellite TV service gave the 201
residents free service for
ten years in exchange for
renaming the town
DISH!

James: What happens when snakeskin cowboy boots get wet?

Anna: They become water moccasins!

TEXAS BIG!

The State Fair of Texas boasts one of North America's tallest Ferris wheels! It's called the Texas Star and it's 216 feet high!

STATUESQUE FACTOID:

Some say Hollywood's Oscar statuette was named after Oscar Pierce, a Texan, who had kin in the movie industry!

★ HOLLYWOOD ★

Oscar Pierce

LAREDO LIBRARY LAFFS!

THE LIFE OF A RODEO COWBOY
BUCK N. BRONCO

TEXAS TEA: I STRUCK IT RICH!
O.L. WELLES

HOW TO DO ROPE TRICKS
by LARRY ETT

Cowboy Cooking
CHRIS P. BACON

INFAMOUS TEXAS BAD GUYS
BY ROBIN BANKS

CLASSIC TEXAS MOVIES
by Wes Tern

EVERYTHING'S BIGGER IN TEXAS
by Hugh Japlace

When Yer Cows Act Bad
Terry Bull

HAPPY TRAILS TO YOU
BY DUSTY RHODES

THE TOP TEN:

CATTYWAMPUS COOKIN' AT THE TEXAS STATE FAIR!

Texas State Fair

10. Fried Jell-O

9. Funnel cake bacon queso burger

8. Deep-fried Snickers

7. Fried spaghetti and meatballs

6. Fried root beer

5. Deep-fried Froot Loops

4. Chicken noodle soup on a stick

3. Kool-Aid marinated pickles

(Texas children's librarian, Cindy Vela, tells me they're called Koolickles.)

2. Deep-fried bubble gum

And the best (or maybe the worst!):

⭐ 1. Cotton candy tacos ⭐

IF Y'ALL GO HOME HUNGRY IT'S YER OWN FAULT!

CRAFTY FACTOID

Black Texan civil rights activist Juanita Craft, who fought for desegregation of the University of Texas Law School and the Texas State Fair, was invited to the White House by three U.S. presidents!

Knock? Knock?
Who's there?

Juanita Craft!
Juanita Craft who?

Juanita Craft civil rights laws!

HIGHWAY SNOBBERY!

Texans are proud of many things—including their highways! They have more than 70,000 miles of them and use 1.6 million gallons of paint every year to paint the lines on them!

What was the turtle doing on the famous Route 66 in Texas?

About 16 inches per hour!

OFFICIALLY FUNNY!

OFFICIAL

The Official Texas State Dog:

Blue Lacy

What did the cowboy say when his Blue Lacy ran away?

Dog-gone! ARF! ARF!

The Official Texas State Flower:

Bluebonnets

also called wolf flower, buffalo clover, and *el conejo* (that's "rabbit" in Spanish).

What does a bee call a bluebonnet?

HONEY!

The Official Texas State Motto:

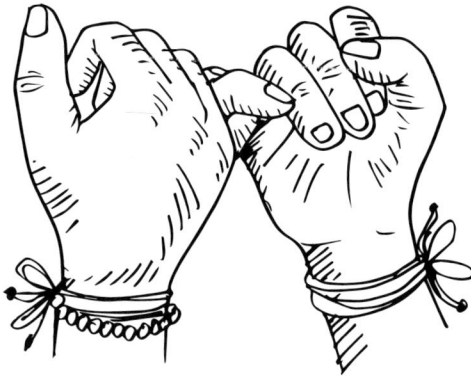

Friendship

Melissa: What do bluebonnets call their best friend?
Finn: BUD!

OFFICIAL

The Official Texas State Reptile:

Texas Horned Lizard

What do you call a Texas horned lizard that likes hip-hop?
A **RAP**-tile!

OFFICIAL

The Official Texas State Plant:

Prickly Pear Cactus

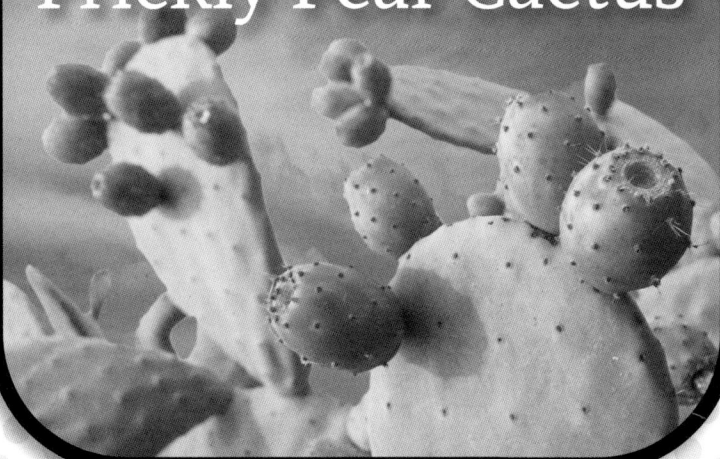

What did the baby porcupine say to the cactus?

"Is that you, Mama?!"

The Official Texas State Bird:

Mockingbird

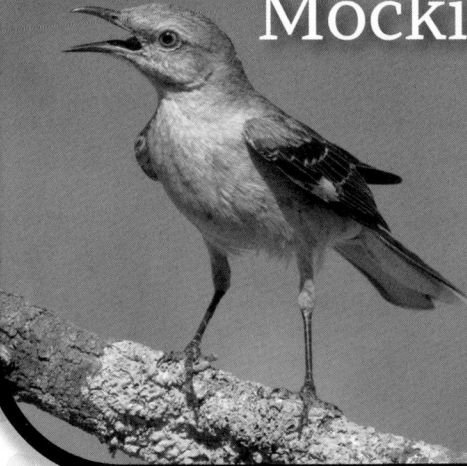

Peggy: Why did the mockingbird cross the road?

Mickey: Why did the mockingbird cross the road?

Peggy: Ok, seriously what do you call a mockingbird's son?

Mickey: A CHIRP off the old block! LOL!

The Official Texas State Song:

"Texas, Our Texas"

Tex: Y'all should sing "Texas, Our Texas" solo!

Rex: Aw, shucks, really?!

Tex: Yup, **so low** I can't hear yuh!

The Official Texas State Fruit:

Red Grapefruit

Why did the red grapefruit go to the doctor?

It wasn't **peeling** well!

The Official Texas State Tree:

Pecan

KNOCK! **KNOCK!**

Who's there?

Pecan!

Pecan who?

Pecan in yer window and saw that you were home, so we can chaw the rag!

The Official Texas State Nickname:

OFFICIAL

The Lone Star State

I'm so lonely. Boo hoo.

The Official Texas State Dinosaur:

Brachiosaurus

**What do you call a
Brachiosaurus in high heels?**

A My-feet-are-**saur**-us!

The Official Texas State Vegetable:

Sweet Onion

Why will the sweet onion laugh at this here joke?

To keep from crying! :'(

OUT OF THIS WORLD FACTOID

The first song broadcast from outer space was "San Antonio Rose," by Bob Wills and the Texas Playboys. The song, recorded in Dallas, was on a mix tape that belonged to astronaut Pete Conrad, who took it with him on his Apollo 12 mission (in 1969).

Neil: Did you hear about the Texas Longhorn astronaut?

Buzz: Yup, it went to the **MOOOO**-n!

NO WOOL BULL!

Texas produces more wool than any state in the union!

What do you call a Texas sheep that stinks?

A p-**EWE**!

Ovejita: ¡Mamá!, ¡Mamá! ¿Puedo ir a una fiesta?
Mamá oveja: Veee, veee!

LAFF IN THE FAST LANE!

The United States' fastest road, where y'all can drive faster than a sneeze through a screen door, is a 40-mile stretch between Austin and San Antonio. The legal speed limit is 85 miles per hour!

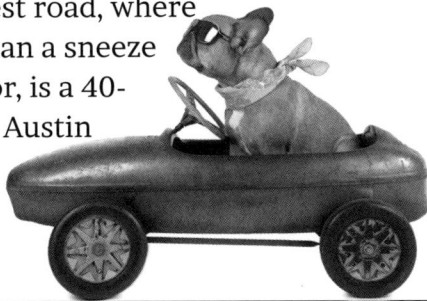

Mike:
How do you measure the speed of an LOL Texas joke?

Nancy:
Tell me!

Mike:
In *SMILES* per hour!

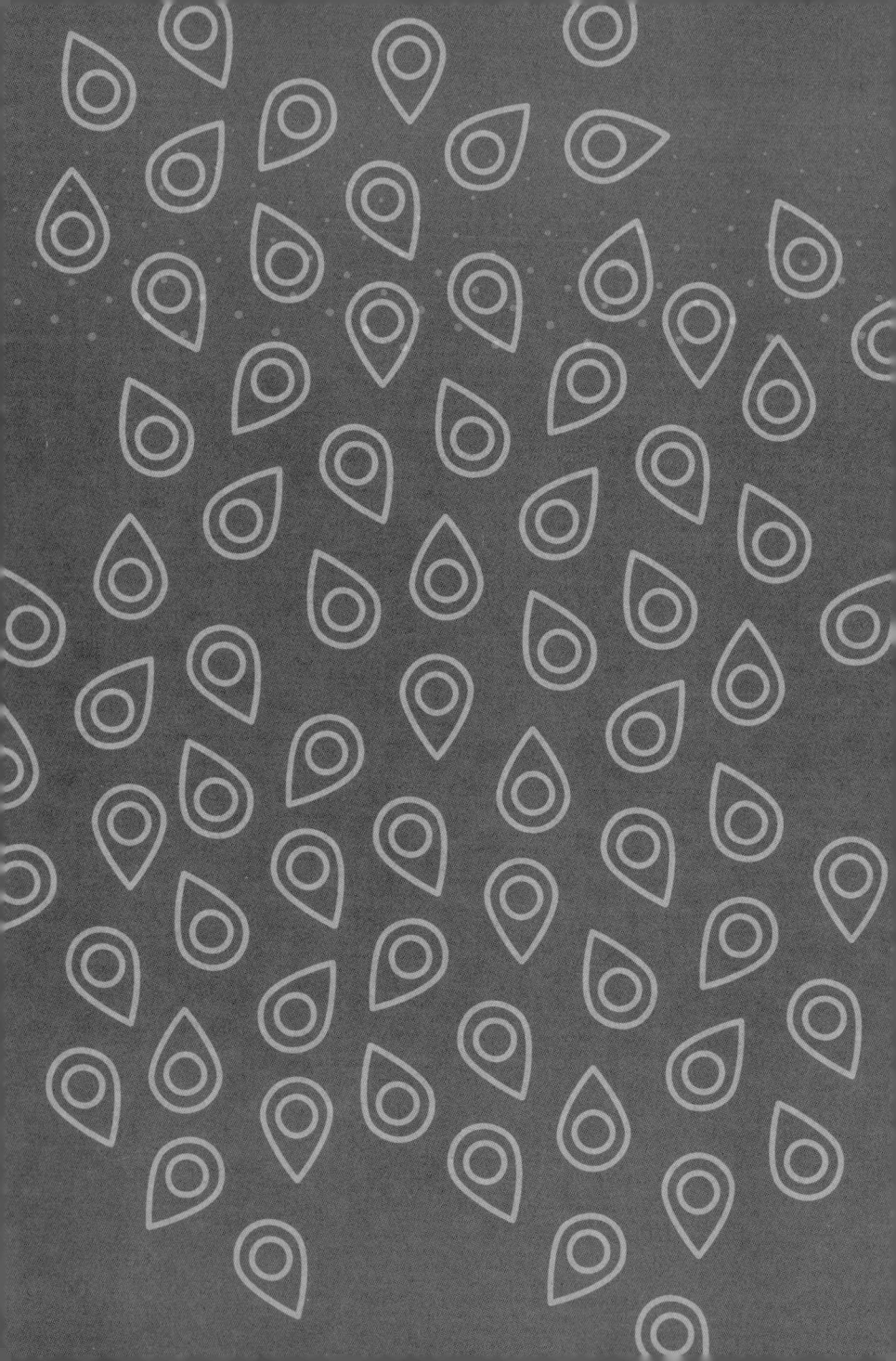

FUN FACTOID

Hola y'all, everything's bigger in Texas! In fact, the Texas State Capitol building is 23 feet taller than the U.S. Capitol in Washington, DC!

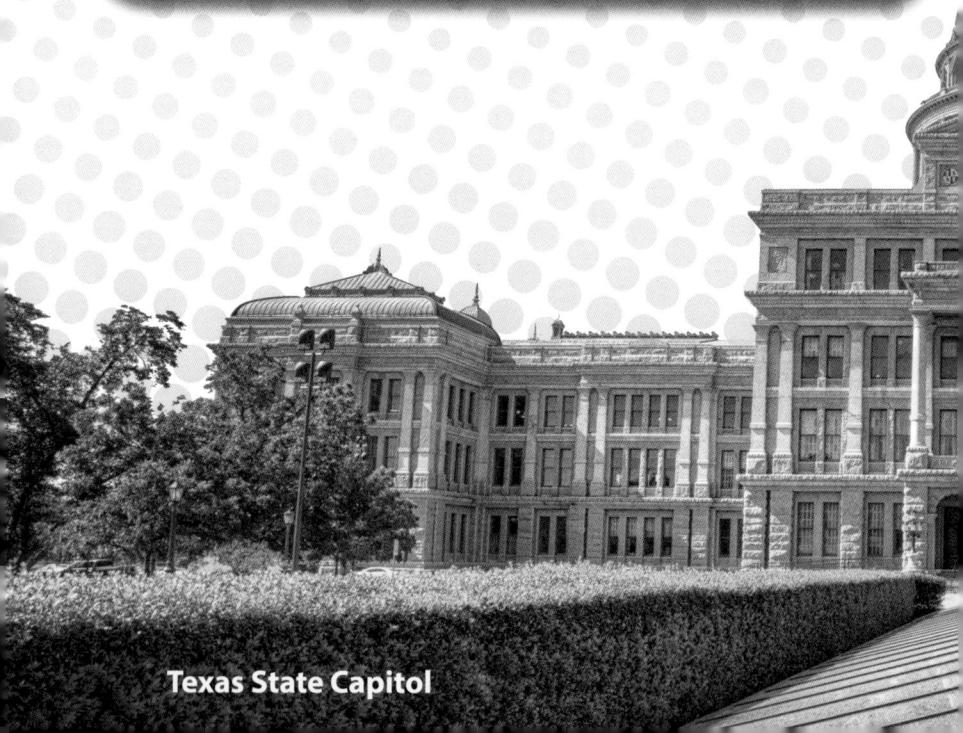

Texas State Capitol

Kate: Which member of the Bigger family from Austin is bigger—Dad Bigger, Mom Bigger, or Baby Bigger?

Chris: Dad Bigger?!

Kate: Baby Bigger! She's just **A LiTTLE** Bigger!

The Dallas Children's Hospital had a wonderful model train display with U.S. landmarks including Mount Rushmore, the Grand Canyon, and the Dallas skyline!

What's the difference between a teacher and a train?

A teacher says,

"Spit out yer gum,"

and a train says,

"CHEW! CHEW!"

A HAIRY SITUATION!

HAIRY MAN RD

A Bigfoot-type beast supposedly lives in the Austin-Round Rock metro area! He's called Hairy Man and allegedly lives on Hairy Man Road.

Q: Which side of Hairy Man is the hairiest?

A: The OUTside!

Plane Crazy!

The Dallas/Fort Worth airport is larger than New York City's Manhattan Island. DFW airport also boasts one of the world's most ginormous parking lots!

Gracie: My mother just flew in to visit me!

Griffin: Nice! Did you meet her at the airport?

Gracie: Goodness gracious, no! I've known her all my life!

BANK ON THIS!
Tired of standing in lines at the bank, Dallasite Donald Wetzel patented the ATM in 1969!

Mac: I don't understand why the ATM doesn't dispense coins.

Zac: Yeah, it doesn't make **CENTS**!

HOUSTON, WE HAVE A MOON ROCK!

At Space Center Houston, you can get a behind-the-scenes tour of NASA, watch astronauts train for their missions, and touch a moon rock!

WHY IS A MOON ROCK TASTIER THAN AN EARTH ROCK?

BECAUSE A MOON ROCK IS A LITTLE METEOR! (MEATIER!)

JUNKY FACTOID!

In the late 1980s, Vince Hanneman started piling up pieces of scrap in his backyard: bottles, air conditioners, bicycle frames, lawn mower parts, and much, MUCH more. Today, his Cathedral of Junk in Austin is a popular tourist destination!

Cathedral of Junk

CROSS THIS BRIDGE WHEN YOU GET THERE!

Built in 1870, the Waco Bridge that crosses the Brazos River in Waco, Texas, was the first major suspension bridge in Texas.

Pedro: ¿Cuánto cuesta el bus?
Conductora: ¡Dos dólares!
Diego: ¡Vale, que se bajen todos los pasajeros que lo compro!

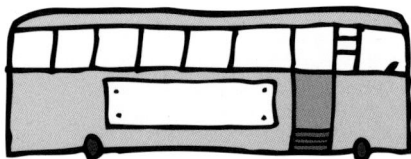

WACKO WACOiTE: Doctor, Doctor, I think I'm the Waco Bridge!

DOCTOR: What's come over you?!

WACKO WACOiTE: Six cars, fifty-eight pick-up trucks, one tractor, and three coyotes!

Waco Bridge

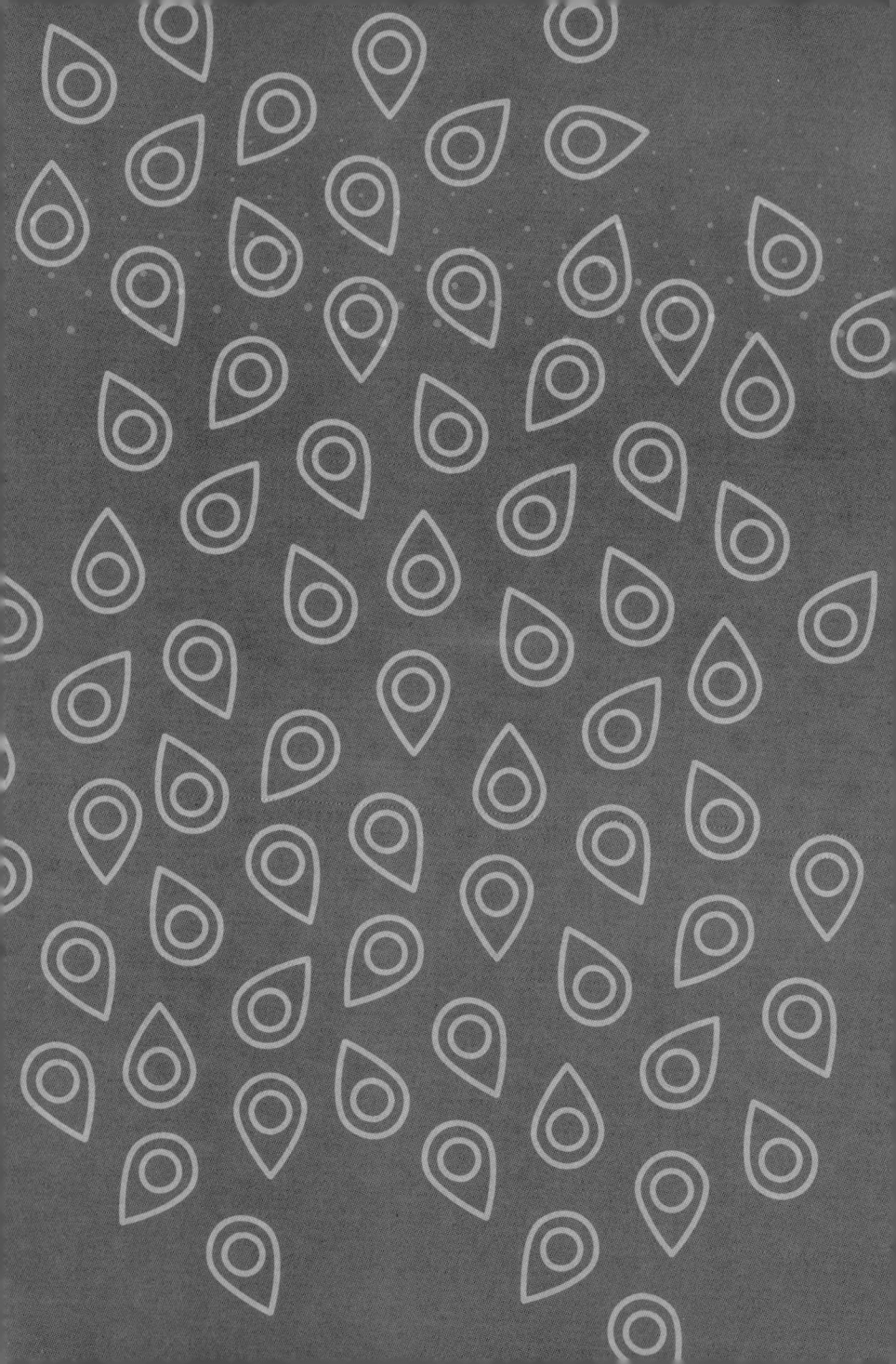

You can visit these food-named towns when looking for some Texas eats:

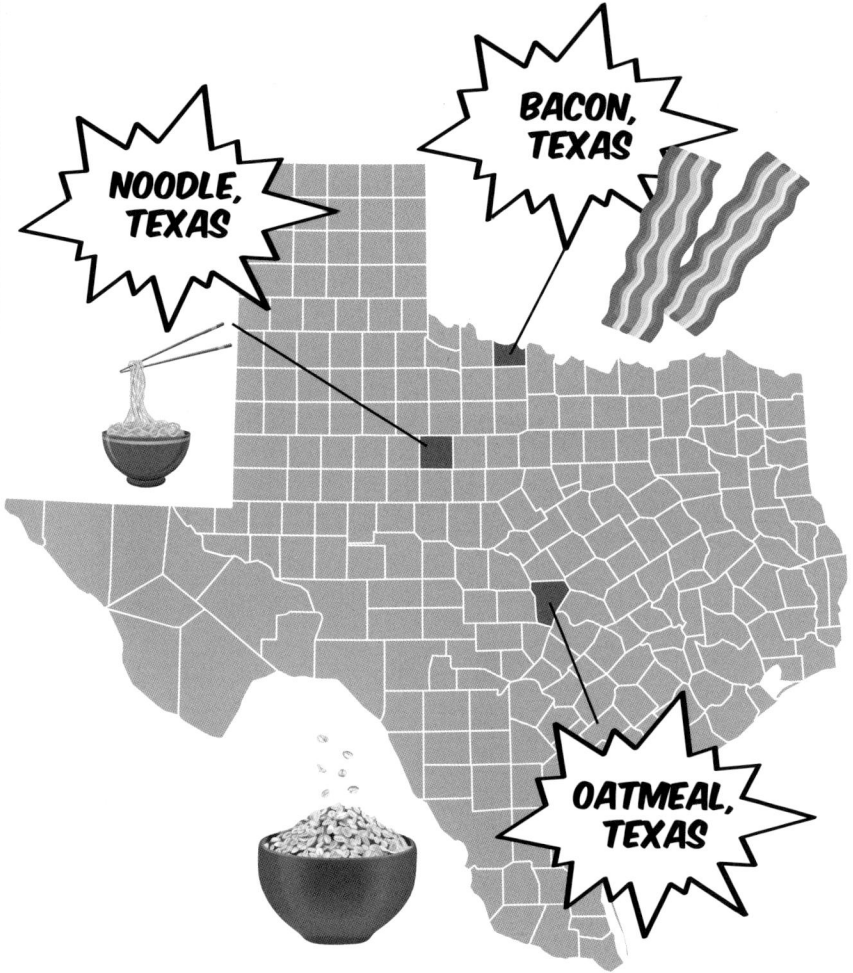

NOODLE, TEXAS

BACON, TEXAS

OATMEAL, TEXAS

BRAIN FREEZE

If you like ice cream (and who doesn't?), when ordering pie in San Antonio holla to the waiter: "REMEMBER THE À LA MODE!"

Hey cowboy, what's yer favorite thang to put on yer salad?

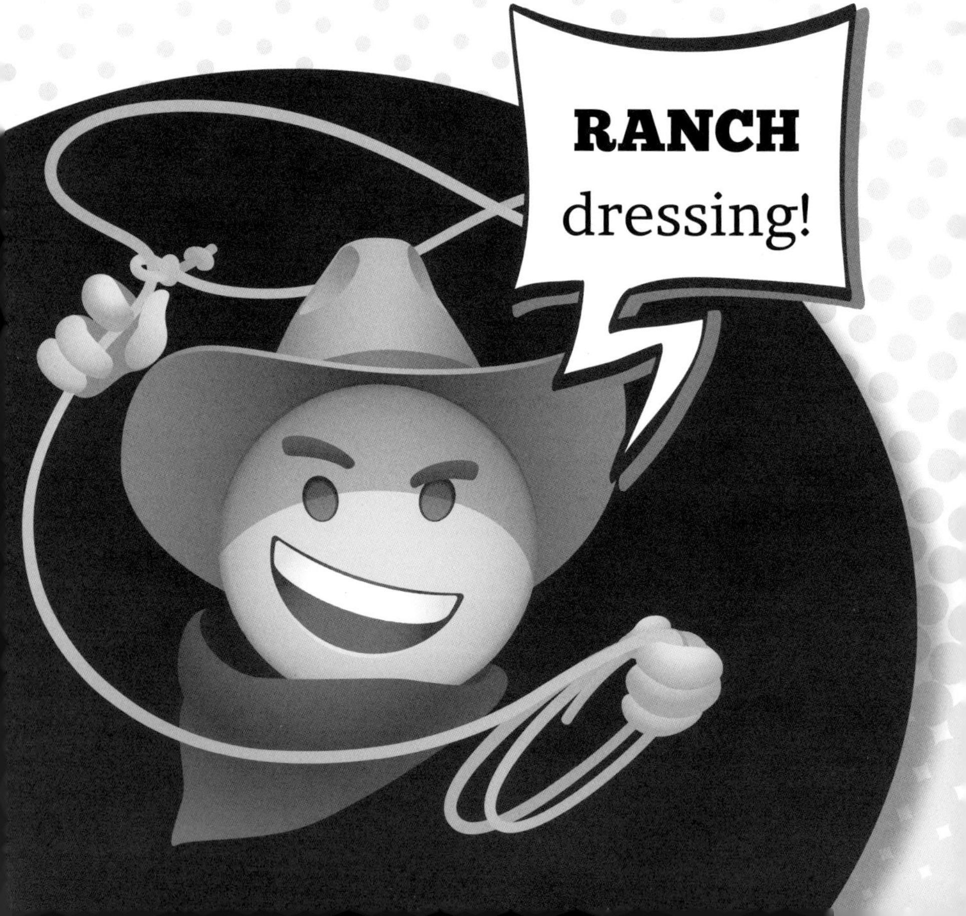

THIS HERE TAKES THE CAKE!

German chocolate cake is not German, but was named after American cake maker Samuel German! The first recipe for German chocolate cake was published in 1957 in *The Dallas Morning News* newspaper. It was the recipe of the day!

There were two pieces of German chocolate cake in the icebox and now there's only one! Can you explain that?!

I didn't see the other one!

BBQ LOL!

Texas, perhaps more than any other state, is big on barbecue!

Why did the Texan stand on a ladder to serve the barbecue, sir?

He wanted the steaks to be high, ma'am!

I hear you threw a barbecue!

Yup, 46 feet!

What's a librarian's favorite thing to eat at a Texas BBQ?

SHUSH KABOB!

Flight instructor:

Congrats, you're just about to get your wings!

Almost pilot:

Honey mustard or barbecue?!

Why did the skeleton go to the barbecue?

To get **ANOTHER RiB.**

What do leprechauns love to barbecue?

Short ribs, sir!

What happened to the Dallasite who showed up late to the Fort Worth barbecue?

She got the
COLD SHOULDER!

Bill:

Why is barbecue so popular in Texas, but not so much in Italy?

Jennifer:

Because the spaghetti keeps falling through the grill!

TEX-MEX MIRTH!

The Latinx influence on Texas is huge (just like Texas!). The most delish vittles in the world are Tex-Mex, the very popular combo of foods and flavors from **TEX**as and **MEX**ico!

What do ya'll call a tortilla chip that works out?

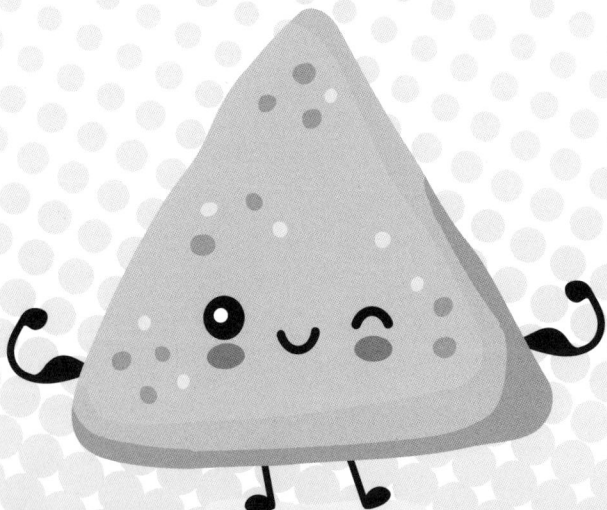

A MACHO NACHO!

What do you call a cat in a blanket?

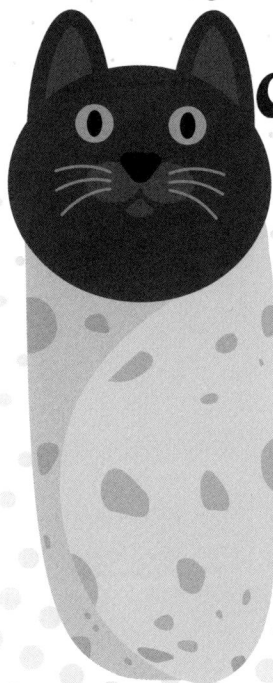

A **PURR-** ito!

I reckon you saw this week's weather forecast?

Sí, it's gonna be cool today, but hot tamale!

What does a sad tortilla say?

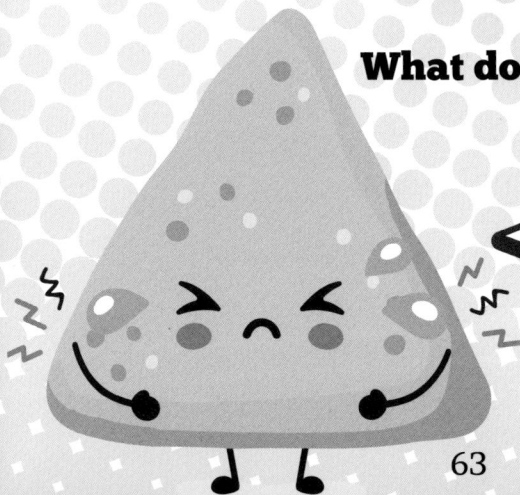

I don't want to TACO 'bout it!

What do you call cheese that isn't yours?

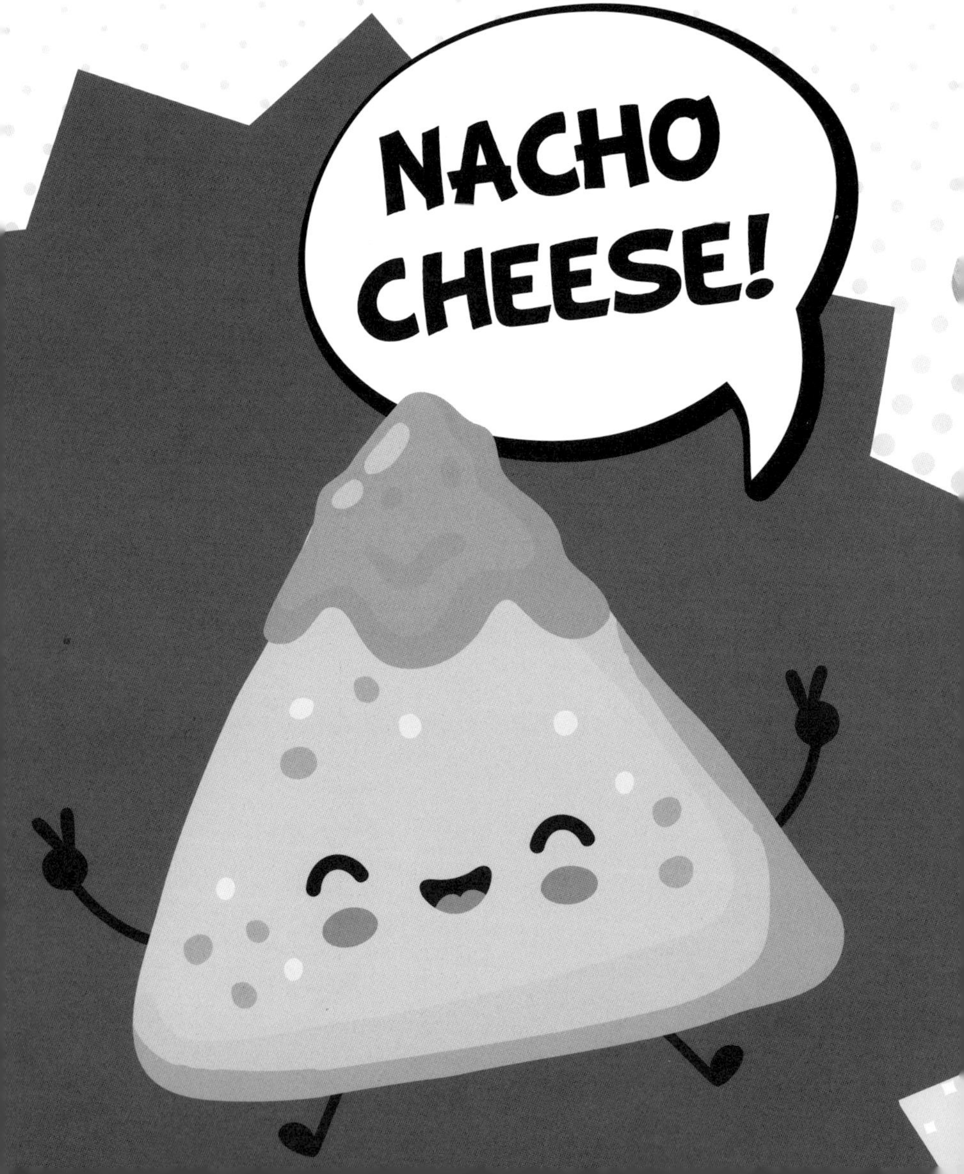

Have you heard my quesadilla joke?
Sí, it's very cheesy.
I admit—it's not so gouda!
Have you heard my tortilla joke?
Sí, it's very CORNY.
Well, I do declare!

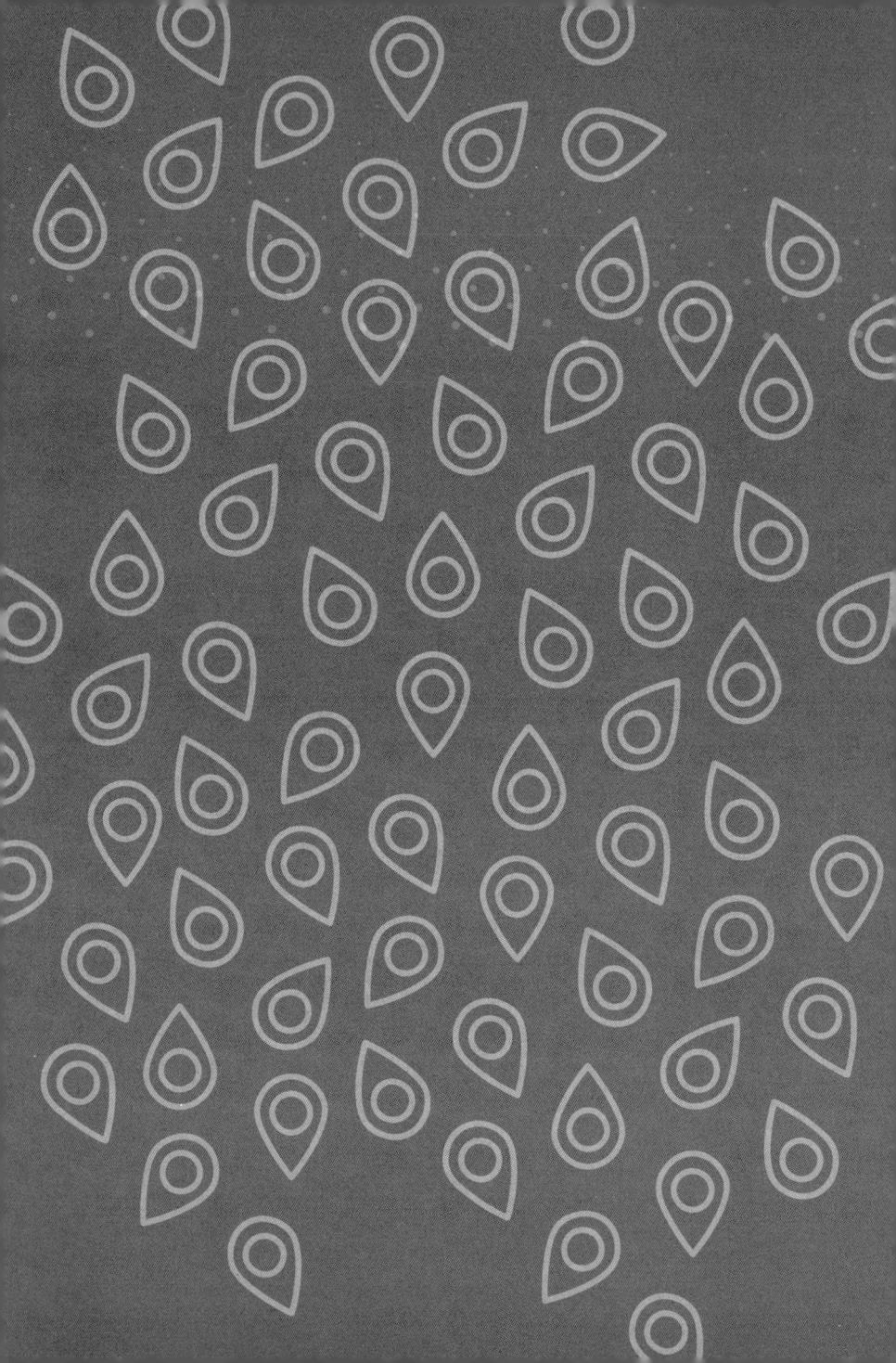

TEXAS IS BATTY!

The largest bat colony in the world is in Texas! Outside of San Antonio is home to more than 20 million Mexican free-tailed bats. That's more than the whole humanoid population of Mexico City!

Bats hanging from the ceiling of Bracken Cave

**Batman:
Where do bats
go to pee?**

Robin:
The **BAT**-room,
duh.

LAUGHING STOCK: TEXAS COW JOKES!

What do you call a Texas cow eating grass?

A lawn MOO-er.

What do Texas cows like to download and watch?

MOO-vies!

KNOCK! KNOCK!

Who's there?

Cow says.

Cow says who?

No, a cow says *MOO*!

What do you call a cow sleeping?

A bull-**dozer**!

Do you want to hear another joke about cattle?

NO!
We already **HERD** enough!

Besides cows and horses, what animal would you like to get on the ranch?

A dachshund— get a **long** little doggie!

HORSING AROUND: TEXAS HORSE JOKES!

What's smarter than a talking horse?

A spelling bee!

What did the mom horse say to the kid horse? **It's pasture bedtime!**

What did the horse say when she finished her lunch?

That was the **LAST STRAW**!

FLUTTER BY THE COCKRELL BUTTERFLY CENTER . . .

. . . at the Houston Museum of Science. The Butterfly Center is a three-story glass enclosure. If you wear bright-colored clothing, some of the over 60 species of free-flying butterflies might land on y'all!

Cockrell Butterfly Center

The Butterfly Center is so beautiful, many people hold their wedding ceremony there!

Why did the crazy-as-a-bullbat boy throw the butter out the window?

He wanted to see BUTTER FLY!

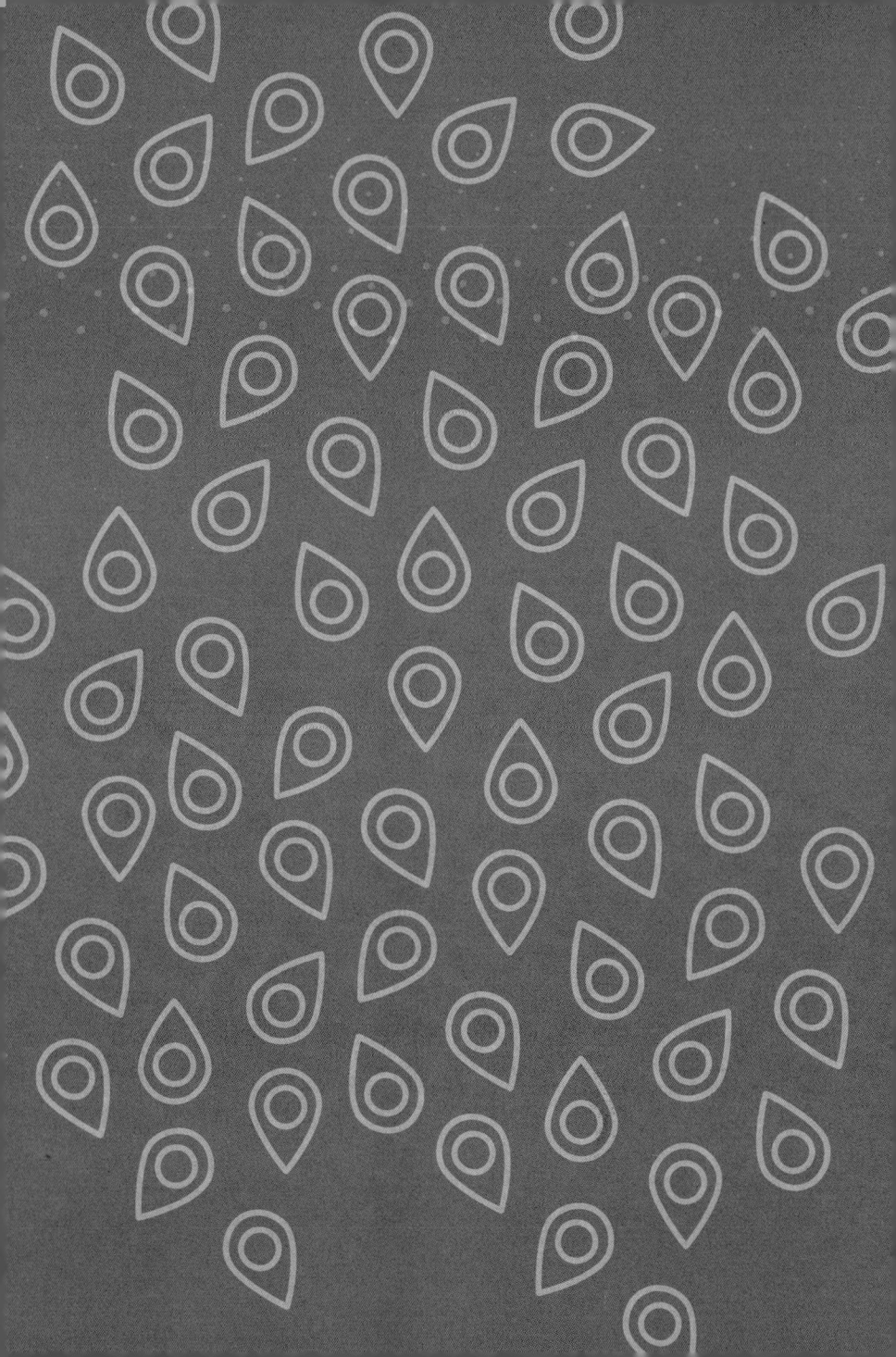

NATURE JOKES

My BFF was Texas cartoonist Gordon "Boody" Rogers. He had a cowboy comic in the very first newsstand comic book, "The Funnies" (1929). Boody turned me on to the beauty of cacti! It's in his memory, I present the following . . .

JOKES WITH A POINT!

What did the cactus say to his BFF?

Boody

Let's **STiCK** together!

Craig

What's worse than dropping yer cactus plant?

Catching it!

Sorry about that.

KNOCK! KNOCK!

Who's there?
Cactus!
Cactus who?
Cactus if you can! :D

KNOCK! KNOCK!

Who's there?
Cactus!
Cactus who?
Cactus makes perfect!

What did the cactus say to the bank teller?

Stick 'em up!

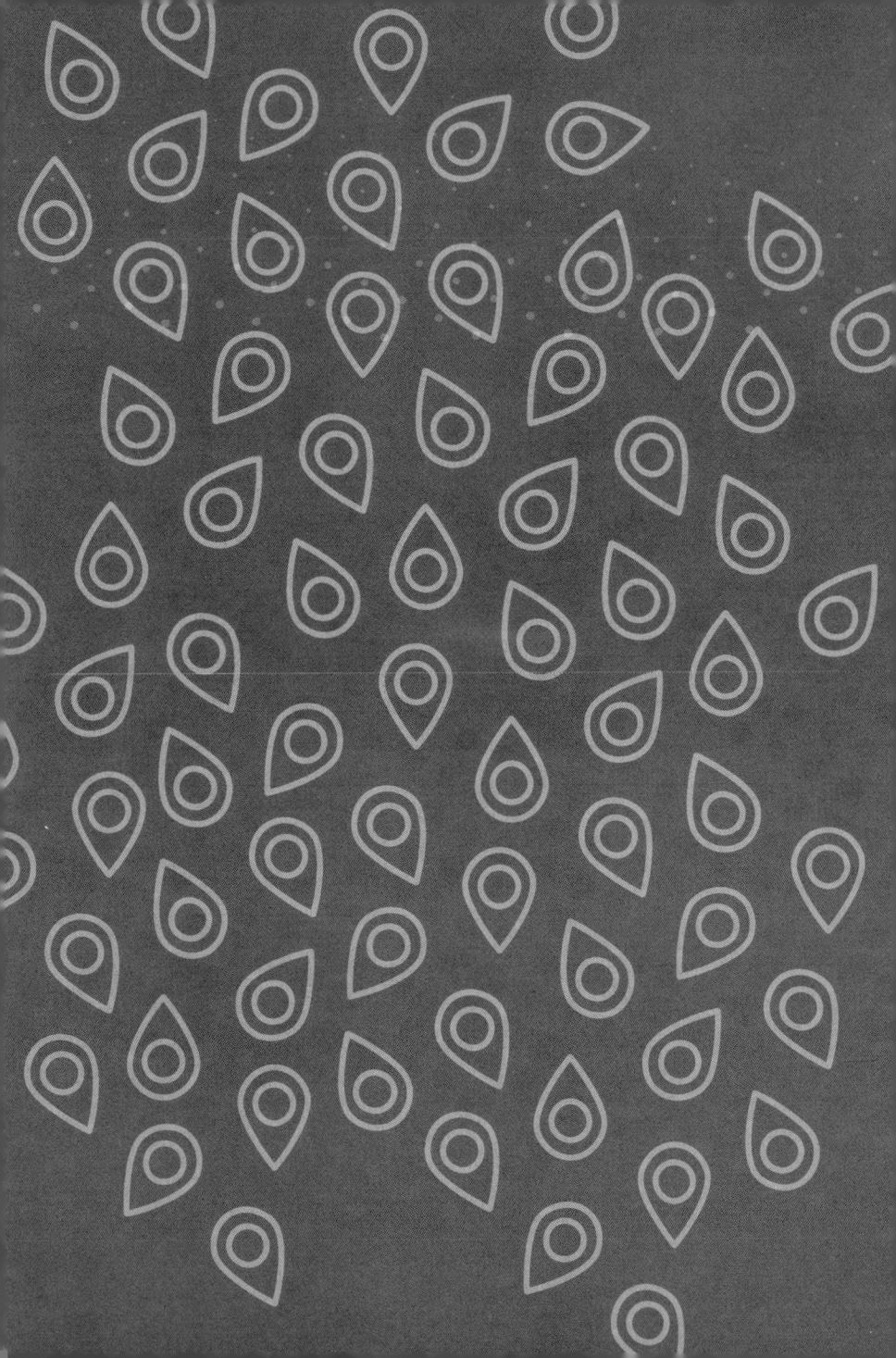

TEXAS SPORTS JOKES
YOU'LL HAVE A BALL, ALL Y'ALL!

What has 18 legs and catches flies?

The Houston Astros!

Why couldn't the Dallas Wings player go on vacation?

No traveling allowed!

What's a zombie's favorite position on the Austin FC team?

Ghoul keeper!

Which Dallas Cowboy has the biggest helmet?

The one with the BiGGEST HEAD!

What do a Dallas Star player and a magician have in common?

They both do hat tricks!

Why did the defensive player for FC Dallas cross the road?

To get to the other **SLiDE!**

Why did the soccer ball quit the Houston Dash team?

It got tired of being kicked around!

Why did the Houston Dynamos do so well in school?

They knew how to use their heads!

What's the Houston Rocket players' favorite cheese?

SWISS!

Get it?!
Swiss!

WHAT DID THE HOUSTON TEXANS PLAYER SAY TO THE FOOTBALL? "CATCH YA LATER!"

Why do the San Antonio Spurs love donuts?

They love to dunk them!

eek!

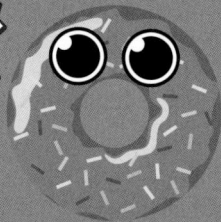

What do Texas Rangers eat their barbecue on?

Home plate! LOL!

THERE'S NO PLACE LIKE DOME!

The NRG Astrodome in Houston was the world's first domed stadium!

Why are the Texas athletes who play at the NRG Astrodome so cool?! Because they have so many FANS!

NRG Astrodome

TEXAS GOOD CHEER!

Cowbelle:

What's our cheering squad's favorite drink?

Beaux:

ROOT beer!

Adios, amigos!